What's in this book

This book belongs to

_____

眼镜在哪里？
Where are the glasses?

学习内容 Contents

沟通 Communication

说说家中的家具和物品
Talk about furniture and objects/items at home

背景介绍：
故事发生前的某一天，爸爸找不到眼镜，全家人帮他一起找，最终浩浩在爸爸卧室的衣橱里发现，眼镜挂在衣服的口袋上。

生词 New words

★	剪刀	scissors
★	报纸	newspaper
★	书架	bookcase
★	沙发	sofa
★	可能	may
★	奇怪	strange
★	又	again

茶几	coffee table
手表	watch
眼镜	glasses
觉得	to think
帮助	to help
衣柜	wardrobe

废物利用，制作收纳盒
Turn a shoe box into a storage box

参考答案：
1 Yes, I could not find my watch this morning./No, I always keep things organized.
2 Yes, I do./No, my room is always messy.
3 He found them perched on the pocket of his father's shirt in the wardrobe.

句式 Sentence patterns

您的眼镜又不见啦？
Are your glasses missing again?

文化 Cultures

中国传统家具
Traditional Chinese furniture

Get ready

1 Have you ever lost something at home?

2 Do you keep your things organized?

3 Where did Hao Hao finally find his father's glasses?

🎧 01 读一读 Read

参考问题和答案：
1 Why do you think Hao Hao says that the characters are strange? (Each character consists of three of the components.)
2 Do you notice something different about Dad? (He is not wearing his glasses.)

书上的汉字都是由三个相同的部件组成的，且需要与对应的图案连线，浩浩觉得这些汉字很奇怪。

故事大意：
爸爸想戴上眼镜帮浩浩看书里的字，却发现找不到眼镜。于是玲玲和浩浩一起帮爸爸找眼镜。最后，当爸爸找得满头大汗，解开衬衫扣子时，玲玲发现眼镜就挂在爸爸衬衫里面的衣服上。

qí guài
奇怪

"爸爸，您看，这些字真奇怪！三个'木'，三个'口'……"浩浩说。

4

"我来看看。咦，我的眼镜呢？在沙发上吗？"爸爸说。

参考问题和答案：

1 Why is Dad looking for his glasses? (Because he wants to take a look at the characters in Hao Hao's book.)

2 Are Dad's glasses on the sofa? (No, they are not.)

参考问题和答案：
1 Is this the first time that Dad has misplaced his glasses? (No, it is not.)
2 What is on the coffee table? (There is a pair of scissors and a watch.)
3 Are the glasses on the coffee table? (No, they are not.)

"您的眼镜又不见啦？茶几上只有剪刀和手表，没有眼镜。"浩浩说。

shū jià
书架

jué de
觉得

当我们想要表达对一件事的看法，但语气不确定时，可以用"觉得"。如"我觉得她是他的妹妹。"

bào zhǐ
报纸

"我觉得它在报纸下面。"玲玲说。
"我觉得它在书架上面。"浩浩说。

"它可能在衣柜里吗?"浩浩问。
"眼镜在爸爸身上!"玲玲说。

bāng zhù
帮助

参考问题和答案：

1 Why does Hao Hao look worried? (Because he cannot find his Chinese book.)
2 How has Dad helped Hao Hao? (Dad returned the book to Hao Hao.)
3 Why is Ling Ling laughing so hard? (Because she thinks the whole situation is very funny.)

"糟糕，中文书又不见了！"浩浩说。
"在这里。我们互相帮助。"爸爸说。

Let's think

1 Recall the story. Put a tick or a cross. 提醒学生回忆故事，观察第3至8页。

2 Let's tidy/clean up. Put the things where they belong and write the letters. 提醒学生思考每件家具的作用，从而将物品放在合适的地方，并帮助学生养成有序整理与收纳的好习惯。

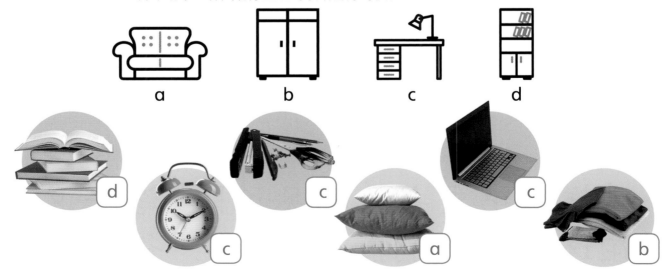

a b c d

d c c c a b

New words

02 **1** Learn the new words.

延伸活动：
老师说出家里的各种房间，如"客厅""书房""卧室"等，让学生尽可能多地说出相应房间里的家具名称，如"客厅里有沙发和茶几。""书房里有书架、书桌和椅子。"

书架

剪刀

觉得

奇怪

手表

报纸

衣柜

可能

又

茶几

沙发

眼镜

帮助

2 Listen to your teacher and point to the correct words above.

听听说说 Listen and say

第一题录音稿：
1 这是我的文具盒，里面有铅笔、橡皮和剪刀。
2 星期日早上，我和姐姐坐在沙发上看书，爸爸戴着眼镜看报纸。
3 爸爸说他的眼镜在衣柜里。你觉得呢？

03 **1** Listen and circle the mistakes.

1

2

3

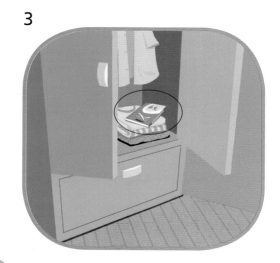

04 **2** Look at the pictures. Listen to the story a

① 今天的报纸来了，爸爸在哪里呢？

他可能又在书房。

剪刀呢？剪刀在哪里？

剪刀在书架上，给你。

12

第二题参考问题和答案：

1 What are Dad and Hao Hao making?
(They are making finger puppets.)
2 Do you like making handicrafts? Why?
(Yes, I think it is interesting./No, I think it is too difficult.)

ly.

咦，这些是什么？真奇怪！

你觉得它们像什么呢？

小恐龙太可爱了！

我觉得你也很可爱！

3 **Write the letters and say.**

a 帮助　b 衣柜　c 又
d 觉得　e 可能　f 手表

这是我的新 _f_ ，
你 _d_ 好看吗？

谢谢你！

不客气，我
们互相_a_。

我的帽子
_c_ 不见了。

它 _e_ 在
_b_ 里面。

Task

提醒学生在对话练习中尽量用到已学的家具词汇。
建议句式："这是……""你（我）觉得……""……有……"

Draw your living room or bedroom. Talk about it with your friend.

这是我家的新沙发。

沙发和茶几都好看。

这是我的卧室，你觉得好看吗？

Game

游戏方法：
老师随意选择选项中的词汇来读，学生找到对应的家具后，可根据自己喜好涂上颜色，
再在空格中填入正确词汇的字母。

Listen to your teacher and colour the furniture. Then match the correct words to them and write the letters.

a 书架　　b 沙发　　c 床　　d 茶几　　e 衣柜　　f 书桌

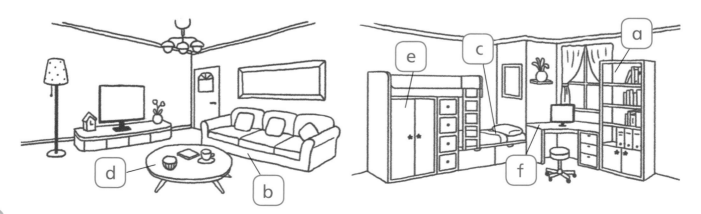

Chant

05 **Listen and say.**
说唱完，让学生在画面中
找一找眼镜在哪里。

眼镜在哪里呀？
眼镜不在报纸下，
也不在沙发上。
真奇怪呀真奇怪！

眼镜在哪里呀？
它可能在书架上，
也可能在衣柜里。
眼镜又跑去哪儿了？

生活用语 Daily expressions

真奇怪!
So strange!

我帮你。
Let me help you.

我们可以说"帮"，也可以说
"帮助"。"帮"更口语化。

15

写一写 Write

1 Trace and write the characters.

ㄱ 又

又　又　又　又

又

提醒学生注意"又"字的笔画，先写横撇，再写捺。

一　丁　丁　可

乙　ㄥ　广　片　自　自　自　能　能　能

可 能　可 能

可 能

提醒学生"能"字右边的部件是"匕"不是"七"。

2 Write and say.

这 <u>可 能</u> 是爸爸的眼镜。

昨天　今天

今天中午，我 <u>又</u> 吃了很多水果。

16

答题技巧：
第一空应填时间，故是"早"。第二空从上下文可知，"我"在周六依旧七点起床准备去上学，
故用"又"。剩下的四个空都是词语和句子的固定搭配，根据语境可以填出。

3 Fill in the blanks with the correct words. Colour the alarm clocks in the same colours.

黄色

橙色

蓝色

绿色

粉色

今天 早 上，我 又 七点起床。洗

脸、刷牙、穿 衣服 ，还找文具盒。

妈妈问："你 想 做什么？"

我说："我去 学 校。"

"今天是星期六，不用上 学 。"妈妈说。

拼音输入法 Pinyin input

Type the missing words to complete the sentences. Number the sentences to make it a meaningful paragraph.

3 但是我胖胖的，很 <u>可爱 keai</u> 。

1 你好，我的 <u>名字 mingzi</u> 叫熊猫。

2 我的身体只有 <u>黑 hei</u> 色和 <u>白 bai</u> 色。

4 快来 <u>动物园 dongwuyuan</u> 找我吧！

排序技巧：
从第二话框的关键词"你好"和"名字"来看，这句是熊猫自我介绍，应为第一句。第一、三话框介绍外貌特点，其中第一话框的"但是"表示转折，所以这两个话框分别是第二、三句。第四话框告诉读者哪里可以找到自己，应是最后一句。

多元学习 Connections

Cultures

1 Traditional Chinese furniture has a long history and rich cultural style. What do you think?

Classical Chinese furniture is mostly made of wood, and built without any glue or nails.

衣柜

书架

书桌

椅子

沙发

茶几

2 Look at the pictures below and talk about them with your friend.

我觉得沙发很舒服。

我喜欢……

这个沙发很好看。

古代中国多用木制的椅凳和榻类。19世纪中期，以沙发为代表的西方家具开始在中国流行。"沙发"一词也从英语sofa音译过来，传入中国。

Project

1 Turn a shoe box into a storage box.

材料：
一个废旧鞋盒（或纸盒）、一张硬卡纸、两张彩色包装纸、一把剪刀、一支笔、一根尺子、一卷透明胶带。

①

③ 制作储物盒的间隔。用尺子量出盒子的宽度和深度。

② 用包装纸将盒子及盖子的外侧包好。

⑥ 将剪好的硬卡纸放入纸盒中，卡纸两侧的空间大小可根据自己喜好进行调节。

⑤

④

剪下画好的长方形。

在硬卡纸上画出相应尺寸的长方形间隔。

⑦

2 Tell your friend where the storage box is and what items it stores.

学生拿着做好的收纳盒讨论，会放在家里的哪个位置，以及会收纳什么东西。

它在我的卧室……

它里面有玩具熊、羽毛球、手表……

游戏方法：
浩浩和布朗尼来到了一个陌生的房间，让学生按照数字顺序，和他们一起边指着家具/物品边说句子。其中第1至7题是说出完整的中文句子，第8题是写字。

1 Hao Hao and Brownie are in an unfamiliar room. Say the sentences to describe the room to them. Then write in the boxes.

5 这是什么画？它真奇怪！

4 书架上有书。

6 沙发真大，可以坐很多人。

3 报纸在桌子上。

7 茶几上有剪刀和手表。

2 我也觉得它很大。

8 树 可 能 不是真的。

1 我觉得这个房间很大，也好很看。

评核方法：
学生两人一组，互相考察评价表内单词和句子的听说读写。交际沟通部分由老师朗读要求，学生再互相对话。如果达到了某项技能要求，则用色笔将星星或小辣椒涂色。

2 Work with your friend. Colour the stars and the chillies.

Words	说	读	写
剪刀	☆	☆	🌶️
报纸	☆	☆	🌶️
书架	☆	☆	🌶️
沙发	☆	☆	🌶️
可能	☆	☆	☆
奇怪	☆	☆	🌶️
又	☆	☆	☆
茶几	☆	🌶️	🌶️
手表	☆	🌶️	🌶️
眼镜	☆	🌶️	🌶️

Words and sentences	说	读	写
觉得	☆	🌶️	🌶️
帮助	☆	🌶️	🌶️
衣柜	☆	🌶️	🌶️
您的眼镜又不见啦？	☆	🌶️	🌶️

Talk about furniture and things at home	☆

3 What does your teacher say?

评核建议：
根据学生课堂表现，分别给予"太棒了！(Excellent!)"、"不错！(Good!)"或"继续努力！(Work harder!)"的评价，再让学生圈出左侧对应的表情，以记录自己的学习情况。

My teacher says ...

分享 Sharing

延伸活动：
1 学生用手遮盖英文，读中文单词，并思考单词意思；
2 学生用手遮盖中文单词，看着英文说出对应的中文单词；
3 学生三人一组，尽量运用中文单词分角色复述故事。

Words I remember

剪刀	jiǎn dāo	scissors
报纸	bào zhǐ	newspaper
书架	shū jià	bookcase
沙发	shā fā	sofa
可能	kě néng	may
奇怪	qí guài	strange
又	yòu	again
茶几	chá jī	coffee table
手表	shǒu biǎo	watch

眼镜	yǎn jìng	glasses
觉得	jué de	to think
帮助	bāng zhù	to help
衣柜	yī guì	wardrobe

Other words

咦	yí	(exclamation of surprise)
糟糕	zāo gāo	too bad
互相	hù xiāng	mutually

OXFORD
UNIVERSITY PRESS

Oxford University Press is a department of the University of Oxford.
It furthers the University's objective of excellence in research, scholarship,
and education by publishing worldwide. Oxford is a registered trade mark of
Oxford University Press in the UK and in certain other countries

Published in Hong Kong by
Oxford University Press (China) Limited
39th Floor, One Kowloon, 1 Wang Yuen Street, Kowloon Bay,
Hong Kong

© Oxford University Press (China) Limited 2017

The moral rights of the author have been asserted

First Edition published in 2017

Illustrated by Anne Lee, KK Ng, KY Chan and Wildman

Photographs for reproduction permitted by Dreamstime.com

China National Publications Import & Export (Group) Corporation is an authorized distributor of
Oxford Elementary Chinese.

Please contact content@cnpiec.com.cn or 86-10-65856782

ISBN: 978-0-19-047007-4

10 9 8 7 6 5 4 3 2

Teacher's Edition
ISBN: 978-0-19-082315-3
10 9 8 7 6 5 4 3 2